2

3

Contents

© 1986 by T.F.H. Publications, Inc. Distributed in the UNITED STATES by T.F.H. Publications, Inc., 211
West Sylvania Avenue, Neptune City, NJ 07753; in CANADA by H & L Pet Supplies Inc., 27 Kingston Cres-
cent, Kitchener, Ontario N2B 2T6; Rolf C. Hagen Ltd., 3225 Sartelon Street, Montreal 382 Quebec; in ENG-
LAND by T.F.H. Publications Limited, 4 Kier Park, Ascot, Berkshire SL5 7DS; in AUSTRALIA AND THE
SOUTH PACIFIC by T.F.H. (Australia) Pty. Ltd., Box 149, Brookvale 2100 N.S.W., Australia; in NEW ZEA-
LAND by Ross Haines & Son, Ltd., 18 Monmouth Street, Grey Lynn, Auckland 2 New Zealand; in SINGA-
PORE AND MALAYSIA by MPH Distributors (S) Pte., Ltd., 601 Sims Drive, #03/07/21, Singapore 1438; in
the PHILIPPINES by Bioi-Research, 5 Lippay Street, San Lorenzo Village, Makati Rizal; in SOUTH AFRICA
by Multipet Pty. Ltd., 30 Turners Avenue, Durban 4001. Published by T.F.H. Publications, Inc. Manufactured
in the United States of America by T.F.H. Publications, Inc.

A Beginner's Guide to
Tropical Fish

Dedicated to my dear friend
Evgeny Semenikhin.
Dr. Herbert Richards

Tropical fish keeping has many advantages over the keeping of other pets. For one thing a tank of fish takes up very little room; a space of only two or three square feet is ample to accommodate an aquarium containing maybe thirty fishes. The cost of setting up an aquarium is not high and there is rarely need to spend additional money on maintenance. Tropical fish consume only a pinch of food at a time and so the weekly cost of feeding is negligible. Odd jobs such as topping up the water in the tank and removing algae from the front glass take only a few minutes per week. There are also advantages over cold water fishes; tropicals are generally smaller, more brilliant and can be obtained in a much greater diversity of shape and colour, and due to the fact that they live in warm water they are more lively and can be kept in much greater numbers.

You can join any number of tropical fish societies where you can learn a great deal about the hobby by meeting people with the same interest. These societies also hold shows where it is possible to exhibit fish. There are several magazines dealing exclusively with tropical fish keeping which are well worth obtaining. In the following chapters I have included all the basic information the beginner to tropical fish keeping will need. Some aspects such as breeding fish can only be covered very briefly in a book of this size, but since it is a very important part of fish keeping some mention has been made when it relates to the different groups of fishes.

This book therefore is intended as an introduction to the fascinating hobby of tropical fish keeping, and if it encourages the reader to further investigation then it has served its purposes. It is necessary to add that although a great deal can be learned from studying literature on the subject, there is no real replacement for practical experience. Do not be afraid to ask advice from other aquarists; your retailer is often a fund of information, and will almost always be delighted to give you the benefit of his experience.

1.
Equipment

Today by far the most popular type of aquarium is the type called the all-glass aquarium. The "all-glass" characterization is not completely accurate, as straight-sided all-glass tanks have more than just glass in their make-up (some are framed in plastic, for example, and all use silicone rubber cement as their joining agent), but it's useful in distinguishing the "all-glass" tank from its predecessor,

Tiger Barbs, Capoeta tetrazona.

the metal-framed aquarium. Metal-framed aquariums are still offered for sale as second-hand items, but they're not sold in pet or aquarium shops.

All-glass aquariums have a few major advantages over the older metal-framed type. In the first place, they're less expensive. They're also lighter, which makes their handling easier, and of course they can never rust. But an even potentially greater advantage is the fact that they can be left to stand indefinitely without any water in them. That is something that was dangerous to do with the old metal-framed tanks; if a metal-framed tank was emptied out and left dry for any length of time, its cement often dried out and shrank, making the tank leak if it were filled again.

It is always best to obtain an aquarium on the large side as this will be easier to maintain and allow for later expansion without additional expense. The surface area of the tank sould be as large as possible in relation to its volume. A good rule to remember is that the height of the tank should never be much greater, if at all, than its width.

Heating

It is most important to provide reliable heating for your fishes. To do this you will need one or more (depending on the size of your tank) tube heaters and a thermostat. It is possible to buy heaters and thermostats combined, which simplifies the whole thing and reduces the cost. Both heater and thermostat, whether combined or not, are of two main types: completely submersible or partly submersible. Both are equally efficient and easily regulated.

As well as heaters an accurate thermometer is an obvious essential. There are many kinds available made especially for the aquarium. Most of them are the conventional type and float vertically at the surface just the same as a fishing float.

For your own protection, always ensure that any electrical equipment you buy complies with the latest safety regulations.

Lighting

It is important to light your tank correctly; a good balanced light not only shows the fish off to their best advantage but also keeps them in good health, and of course it is absolutely essential for good

Equipment available at your petshop.

plant growth. Ordinary tungsten bulbs can be used perfectly well, or the more expensive (to install) fluorescent lighting which really brings the colour of the fish out. Whichever method of lighting you adopt it is important to position it above the tank correctly. Perhaps the best method is to have the light positioned over the front of the tank so that the rays strike the sides of the fish, which are towards you. Conversely if the light shines from behind the fish they will be in silhouette and the colours lost. Specially shaped hoods are available to house lighting. When using ordinary bulbs it is better to use several of low wattage rather than one of high wattage as several bulbs spread the light more evenly over the tank; it is also less of a strain on the fishes' eyes. Fluorescent lighting gives out a light very similar to natural light and is therefore especially beneficial to the plants. Both tungsten bulbs and fluorescent strip lighting can be used in conjunction with one another to excellent effect. When using strip lighting on its own one should allow ten watts for each square footage of tank area. With bulbs allow twenty-five watts per square foot. If the tank is situated in a room where some natural light is available then clearly the period of artificial lighting can be reduced. The amount of light necessary depends to a large extent on the kind of plants you choose, but an average of ten hours of light per day using artificial light should suit most tanks well.

Covers

Unless the top of your tank is covered by a hood you will need a cover glass. The reason for this is that many tropical fish are good jumpers and would almost certainly end up on the sitting room floor unless a cover is fitted. A cover also reduces the amount of water lost through evaporation.

Aeration

Artificial aeration, though not absolutely essential is certainly beneficial to both plants and fish. All that is needed is a small air pump, some air tubing and a diffuser stone. The system works like this: The pump forces air down to the diffuser stone submerged in the water. The rising stream of air bubbles this creates causes an upward current in the tank. This draws water from the bottom of the aquarium, containing much carbon dioxide, to the surface. Here the waste gas is released and oxygen absorbed. The water now passes back down to the base of the aquarium again, thus a continuous circulation of water is produced which keeps the oxygen con-

Equipment available at your petshop.

*A water changer is the single most
important piece of equipment.*

tent of the water high; very little oxygen is absorbed from the bubbles themselves. The great advantage of artificial aeration is that it increases the number of fish a tank can support by 50%. However, do not be tempted, because of this, to bump up the fish population of your tank because if, for instance, the pump breaks down while you are away the fish will soon become affected by the resultant high level of carbon dioxide and correspondingly low level of oxygen. This situation can cause the loss of many fishes.

Filtration

Filters are necessary to keep the tank clean. Once again there are several methods of filtration. The air pump we spoke of can be used in conjunction with a filtration system, and this is a very popular method. The filters operate within the aquarium and function by means of the air lift. This is simply a vertical tube fitted to the filter through which the water is drawn by a stream of tiny air bubbles, thus a current of water is produced through the filter. One of the most widely used types of filter consists of a box packed with nylon wool. The air lift tube is positioned in the centre of this box and fits into the middle of a plastic grid. Water passes through slots at the top of the filter box and is filtered down through the nylon wool as it makes its way to the base of the air lift tube where it escapes. A layer of activated charcoal is often added to these filters to absorb toxic gases.

The Diatom filter works on diatomaceous earth and makes water sparkling clear.

*The Penn-Plax undergravel filter is
exposed for this photo. Normally it
is completely covered with gravel.*

A more recent innovation is the undergravel or biological filter. This consists of a raised perforated plate, usually of corrugated plastic, which lies beneath the gravel with an air lift tube at one corner. The action of this air lift draws water through the gravel which itself acts as the filter media. Minute particles of waste matter are broken up biologically by the bacteria in the gravel as they are drawn down into it. This system is simple, inexpensive and effective.

No matter what type of filtration is used the aquarist should make occasional—once or twice a week, say—changes of some of the water in the tank. It's a very good practice to exchange about 25% of the water each week, replacing waste-laden water with fresh water. Pet shops sell devices that make the exchanges automatically.

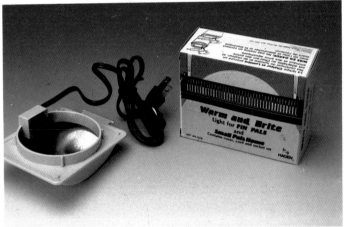

These products are available at your petshop.

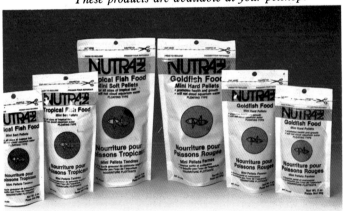

Nets

It is a good idea to purchase at least two nets and to use one in conjunction with the other; fish will often dash into the second net to avoid the first. Fish can also be caught with a net against the glass. Nets should be rectangular rather than circular otherwise you will find it impossible to catch fish which swim into the corners of the tank. A net size of 12 x 10 cm is perhaps the most versatile. A soft nylon netting is kinder to the fish than the conventional mesh.

A scraper for removing algae from the inside glass is another useful item. It is better to use one with a plastic cutting edge rather than a razor blade so as to avoid scratching the glass. On no account use wire wool for the same reason.

A very useful, unique product is this Tetra Gravel Cleaner.

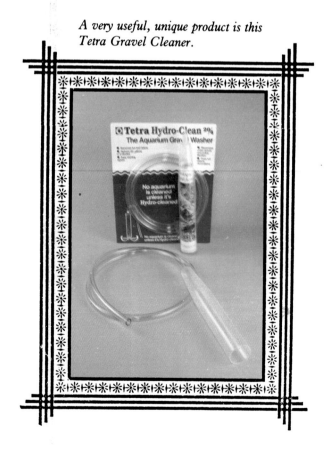

Products which are available at your petshop.

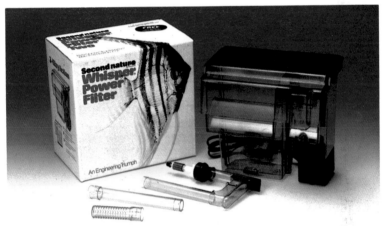

Angelfish and Red Platies in a perfect setting.

2.
Setting up

It is important to remember that when setting up your tank it should be positioned correctly, as once full of water it will be very heavy and extremely difficult to move. The water itself weighs about sixty-two pounds per cubic foot and the sand, rocks and the tank itself will add to this, so make sure also that the stand or table

This is a pair of African Fire Killies, Nothobranchius *species. They only live about a year and are very prolific.*

is strong enough to cope with the load. The tank should be at a convenient height for viewing; about three feet from the floor to base of the tank is best. I would not have the light coming from behind the tank, so do not place the tank with its back to a window. If possible situate it at right angles to the natural light, and make sure that your aquarium is easily accessible for routine maintenance.

To prepare the tank for use it should first be thoroughly washed out with clean warm water (do not use soaps or detergents as these are highly poisonous to fishes) and then filled to the brim and left overnight to test for leaks. Next empty the tank and place it in its final position. It is then ready for the gravel. Suitable aquarium gravel can be purchased in a variety of colours and sizes from any good dealer. The best for general use is 3 to 5 mm washed shingle. The amount needed will be about twelve pounds for each square foot of aquarium base. Although it comes from the dealer already washed, it should nevertheless be washed again before use. A good way to do this is to place the gravel in a bucket and place this beneath a tap on which has been fitted a short length of hose. The hose should be pushed into the gravel right down to the bottom and the tap turned on. With the help of your hand the gravel can be churned up enough to give it a thoroughly good washing. The clean gravel can now be spread over the base of the tank. Try to form a fairly even slope from the back down to about an inch at the front, and build up the sides as well so that you end up with a depression in the centre at the front of the tank where sediment will collect, and can easily be syphoned off. You can now sculpture the floor of the tank into hills and valleys or whatever you choose. Perhaps the most pleasing contours are achieved by banking the gravel back in a series of steps. This can be done with rocks or alternatively with strips of glass or plastic which hold the gravel back well and cannot be seen. By this method whole terrains can be built up and faced with stones and rocks to give an extremely pleasing effect. This has the advantage that small plants need not be confined to the front of the tank but can be planted high up on the "steps" near the back. Another advantage is that these terraces tend to encourage the fish to keep to the front of the aquarium where they are well set off by the background. Sometimes rocks standing up on their edges can be used along the back and sides of the tank to good effect. It is best to use natural waterworn rocks or slate. Limestone and other porous rocks should be avoided.

It is important not to disturb your handiwork once the tank has been set up but you are sure to do this if the water is poured straight in. The best way to introduce the water without disturbing things too much is to place a sheet of glass in the tank, angling it from front to back. The water is then poured onto the face of the glass so that it runs smoothly off each side and the bottom. It is best to plant the tank when about three quarters full. Grass-like plants look best in rows and those with feathery leaves in bunches. Remember to plant carefully and correctly. The parts of the plant where the roots begin should be pushed just under the surface of the gravel, about half an inch, and then the remainder of the root is covered as the plant lies in a horizontal position. Rootless plants such as the floating *Cabomba* should be planted in the same way with the lower part of the stems treated as though they were roots. When planting has been completed the tank can be filled to the brim. Now the heating system can be installed. Heaters and thermostats, if separate, should be submerged in a vertical position at the rear corners of the tank, preferably out of sight behind some rocks. It is important that they are not touching each other. Combined heater thermostats should always be placed in an upright position. Special clips are obtainable to hold heaters and thermostats in position. Filters also should be placed at the back of the tank in a concealed position.

It is advisable to let the tank stand for about a week before introducing any fish. During this time the water will "age", become dechlorinated and clear. It will also give the plants time to root themselves, otherwise the fish will easily uproot them. The temperature of the water will have had time to reach a sufficient level and to be adjusted if necessary. Most freshwater tropicals will live quite happily within a temperature range of between 23°C and 26°C.

Now that the tank is set up and tested your first fishes can be purchased. It is best to get them from a reliable dealer who can advise you on the best kinds to begin with. Make sure that whatever you buy are lively with well spread fins and look well fed. Watch out for pinched stomachs, fungus spots on the body or fins, or fish that appear to be swimming labouriously. When transporting your fish home do not subject them to excessive vibration; fish like all other animals are upset by moving. Once home they should not be poured straight into the tank but left in their plastic bags floating in the tank for about half an hour. This allows the temperature of the water inside the bag to reach that of the tank gradually. How-

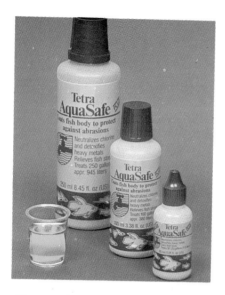

Your petshop will have special water treatment chemicals to help you start your aquarium successfully; ask your dealer's advice.

ever, it may be that the quality of the water may still be different so mix them slowly by dipping the bag, letting a little more enter each time. Finally tip the fish gently into the tank. It is better that these first fishes are selected from the cheaper and hardier varieties, and purchased only a few to begin with, until a little experience has been gained. Most of the species described in this book can be kept together in a so-called community tank. The expression simply means a tank in which several different species are kept together, rather than a number of fish of the same species. Many beginners like to gain the all round experience that a community tank can give, but it must be remembered that not all fish will live peaceably together. As a general rule it is best to keep together fish of a similar size. Different fish swim at different levels in the tank so it is best to collect a good cross section of species to distribute them evenly. Some fish, such as danios, naturally form shoals and therefore look better if kept in numbers.

Maintenance

The general maintenance of the aquarium takes up very little time and is usually just a matter of feeding and checking that everything is in order. The most important thing is to check on the condition of the fish. This is best done at feeding times as fish quickly learn to identify their feeding stations and will rise to the surface in full view to be fed. Watch for fish that show no appetite, are sluggish, have changed to an unusual colour, or have drooping or closed fins. A fish showing any of these symptoms is a clear indication that something is wrong; so check the fish out carefully for signs of disease. Sluggishness of fishes may be a sign of overcrowding. The number of fish you can keep together in one tank is dependent on its surface area. This is because fishes rely on oxygen dissolved at the surface of the water. Too large a number of fish will cause carbon dioxide to build up in the water, which uses up all the space needed for oxygen. As a general guide allow six square inches of surface area for every inch of fish. Fumes such as those from some slow burning stoves and petroleum products can affect the water and are very harmful to fishes, so keep these well away. Many people believe snails to be beneficial to the aquarium. It is true that they will eat algae and any left over food, but they quickly multiply, attacking the growing tips of plants and consuming valuable oxygen, as well as creating more waste products than they consume.

The water in a healthy aquarium stays crystal clear and is practically odourless. A certain amount of brownish sediment is bound to occur on the bottom of the aquarium. Much of this will sink into the gravel to be absorbed by the growing plants. Any excess may be removed with a syphon or by a filtration process. If the gravel becomes blackened it is probably due to rotting food. This will cause a build up of dangerous bacteria and should be rectified immediately.

Although the front glass must be cleared of algae it is beneficial to the fish to leave a little on the back and sides on which they can feed. Algae is essential to the diet of some fishes. The surface of the water may develop an oily appearance. This is easily removed by drawing a piece of newspaper across the surface.

Water lost by evaporation can be replaced with fresh water from the tap. The water temperature should be checked often in case an adjustment to the thermostat is necessary. It is a good idea to keep a spare heater handy just in case. Check that the tank is not over illuminated; if it gets too much light the plant leaves become smothered with thick algae and the water becomes green.

If your tap water comes through copper piping run the tap for several minutes before taking water for the aquarium so that any accumulating copper salts are flushed through. If these salts accumulate in the aquarium they can be very deadly.

The pH (Potential Hydrogen ion) may be either alkaline or acid, depending on the nature of the surrounding soil. You can either buy fish that prefer the pH in your area or change the pH of your tank to suit the fish of your choice. To increase the pH, to make it more alkaline, add sodium bicarbonate; to decrease it, to make it more acid, use sodium acid phosphate. Any change however, must be done gradually and carefully. Many simple pH test kits are available which make it easy to determine the pH of your water. Most fish will, however, adapt themselves fairly readily to the water in your aquarium.

Zebra Danio, Brachydanio rerio.

3.
Feeding

In their natural state tropical fishes feed on small life forms and vegetable matter such as soft water plants and algae. Nature provides a balanced and varied diet and you must endeavour to do the same in your aquarium. The simplest way to provide this is to use a good quality dried food of the kind obtainable from any aquarist store. A dry flaked food is easily broken up by the fishes into parti-

A Marble Veiltail Angelfish.

cles which they can readily consume. The flake can also be broken up for feeding to young fishes. Dried food also takes care of the need for roughage, but care must be taken over the amount of food given as excess will quickly decompose and pollute the water. No more should be fed than can be consumed in five minutes, therefore it is much better to feed little and often; some aquarists feed their fish three times a day, but it is only wise to do this when you know exactly how much they are eating. Most beginners tend to overfeed their fishes. A clear advantage of the dried food product is that it can be stored over long periods.

Fish, like people, appreciate variety in their diet and to keep fish really healthy you much supply a certain amount of live food. One of the best is *Daphnia*. These small crustaceans are often called water fleas due to their flea-like shape and the way in which they hop through the water. They are naturally found in stagnant pools and are most numerous during the late spring-early summer period. They can then be easily purchased in most good aquarium shops. Another live food commercially sold is *Tubifex*. These are small worms which are usually found where sewage is released. Because of this they must be washed thoroughly before feeding to the fish. Unfortunately, they can only be stored for a short time and are best kept in moving water. The best way is to place them in a dish under a constantly dripping tap, but even then they cannot be stored for long. It is always a danger that along with these foods other harmful creatures such as leeches, hydra or carnivorous insect larvae may be introduced into the tank, as well as infectious diseases which may be transmitted to the fishes. A live food which has none of these drawbacks is the white worm (*Enchytraeus albidus*). These little nematode worms can be cultivated by the aquarist to give a continuous supply. To breed them you need a shallow box which should be filled with a mixture of peat and leaf mould in equal amounts. Both of these can be obtained from garden suppliers. The mixture should be watered until it is moist. Now the culture, which you can get from any aquarist, is placed in a depression made in the centre of the compost and a small quantity of food placed on top. Suitable food can be made up with moistened baby cereral, porridge, bread soaked in water or milk, or boiled potato. The worms should be given a constant supply of food, but make sure that any mouldy food is removed. The box should be covered over with glass and kept at a temperature of between 10°C and 15°C. Worms will collect on the glass near the food, and all you have to do when you need some for feeding is to scrape them off with your

An albino suckermouth catfish, Hypostomus.

finger. It is a good idea to break the compost up from time to time so that it is well aerated. Never allow the culture to dry out; dampen it from time to time.

Earthworms provide excellent food for fishes, especially for the larger varieties. For smaller fish the worms can be chopped into manageable sizes.

Other foods which provide a welcome change include lean meat, heart, liver and kidney, shrimp and prawns, crab or lobster, cod roe and white fish meat. A little cheddar cheese may also be appreciated occasionally. Any uneatern food must be removed within twenty-four hours. Most fishes require a certain amount of vegetable matter in their diet. A little algae should be present but this can be supplemented by chopped frozen spinach (de-frozen of course). Some of the larger fishes will enjoy shredded lettuce and the introduction of a little duckweed is beneficial.

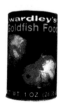

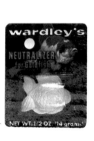

28

Fish fry, especially the egglayers, need very fine particles of food. A good starter food can be prepared from egg yolk. To make this simply rub a small piece of hard boiled egg yolk between the fingers into a jar of water. This fine emulsion can be added to the feeding tank in very small amounts three times a day. Any which is not eaten promotes the growth of infusoria which in turn is a valuable food for fish fry. Infusoria is a collective name for minute protozoa which are found in all tanks in small quantities; these increase when supplied with the kind of food of which we are speaking. Slightly larger fry will take small live food such as brine shrimp. Eggs of brine shrimp are easily obtained and can be hatched in one to two days if placed in water at 26°C, and containing two to three teaspoons of sea salt per pint. A better hatch is obtained if the water is well aerated. A simple hatching unit can be made by cutting the bottom out of an old well washed detergent bottle. Attach an air tube to the nozzle and hang the bottle upside down in a small tank of water kept at 26°C. Next pour a pint of salted water into the bottle plus the eggs to be hatched. The air passing into the bottom of the container will produce a stream of air bubbles which will keep the water in the bottle well aerated and stop any of the eggs from settling on the bottom. When hatched the shrimps are a bright pink/orange colour and can be seen as a cloud in the water. They can now be strained off using a piece of fine cloth which is then simply dipped into the feeding tank to release the shrimp.

Micro-worms which are smaller than white worms are also useful for feeding to fry. Two good culture media for these are porridge or baby cereral mixed with a little water. This should be placed in a small dish about half an inch deep and three to four inches in diameter, and the worm culture added. The dish should be covered with a sheet of glass. After about a week at a temperature of 21°C-25°C the worms will become overcrowded and can be collected from the sides of the container with the finger. The culture medium will now need changing and a new culture started with worms from the old. You will need to have three cultures at different stages to obtan a continuous supply. As fish fry increase in size sifted *Daphnia* or chopped white worms may be used.

On the facing page: These special fishfoods and aquarium aids are available at most petshops.

Your aquarium store might have a magnificent centerpiece for your aquarium. This is Otellia alismoides.

4.
Plants

Plants are a very important part of an aquarium for not only do they provide decoration but also keep the tank clean and healthy. They absorb carbon dioxide and release oxygen, though the amount of oxygen given off is very small in relation to the amount absorbed by the water surface. Much more important are the cover and hiding places they provide for the young fishes and females being pursued by over zealous males. Plants also provide shade and may in-

This beautiful water plant almost never flowers in the home aquarium because it doesn't get enough light. The plant is called Bacopa amplexicaulis.

duce fishes to breed. A large amount of plants in a tank will absorb nearly all the available light and this will tend to keep down the growth of algae. Plants also absorb large quantities of sediment from the gravel, thus helping to keep the tank filtered and clean.

Aquariums are often under planted so remember that in a thickly planted aquarium the water will remain clearer, the tank cleaner, and the fishes healthier.

When planting your aquarium keep the plants well away from the edges, otherwise you will find it extremely difficult to catch fish when you have to.

There are ever increasing numbers of plant varieties available, cerainly too many to include in this book, therefore I have only described the main groups of plants and those more readily available.

Grass-like Plants

Most commonly used are plants of the genera *Vallisneria* and *Sagittaria*. *Sagittaria natans*, when available, is perhaps the toughest of all tropical aquarium plants. It has a large base and is a heavy feeder, absorbing much sediment, and it does not need a lot of light to grow well.

Vallisneria spiralis is very similar but grows more slowly and has longer softer leaves of a lighter colour. It needs a fair amount of light to grow well. Both this and the preceding species may produce small white flowers at the water surface. A second variety of val is often available, *Vallisneria torta*, which has twisted leaves, usually shorter than those of *V. spiralis*. This is a highly decorative species.

Wide Leaved Plants

These include the genera *Ludwigia*, *Hygrophila* and *Nomaphila*. All have conventional leaf shaped leaves.

Ludwigia mulertii needs strong light to grow well. The leaves have coppery undersides. *Hygrophila polysperma* has longer and lighter green leaves. This genus grows faster than *Ludwigia*. *Nomaphilia stricta* is often called Giant Hygrophila to which it is similar but for size; the leaves are darker and much larger.

Left to right: Corkscrew Val, Vallisneria natans *and* Blyxa aubertii. *Plant drawings courtesy of Tropica, Denmark.*

33

Feathery Leaved plants

These provide very good cover for small fishes. *Cabomba* is by far the most popular species, but it does need plenty of light if it is to grow properly. If planted immediately the stems often rot away at the surface of the gravel. It is far better to float the plant for a while until roots develop. (When purchased Cabomba seldom has any roots.) Often these grow up the stem at various points. Chop off any poor stem and plant where the roots are thickest. Also available are *Limnophila sessiliflora*, (ambulia) and *Myriophyllum* (parrot feather). Feathery leaved plants are rather delicate and are therefore not suitable for tanks containing some of the larger fish varieties, especially barbs. The genus *Cryptocoryne* contains many very useful plants which mainly prefer shady positions and can be planted in dark corners of the tank. There are several very small species such as *Cryptocoryne nevilli* which only grow to about two inches and are therefore very suitable for planting at the front of the tank. Another low growing species is *C. beckettii* which has spear shaped pale green leaves which usually lie horizontally making the height of the plant only about one and a half inches. *C. ciliata* is a much taller variety with leaves rising horizontally to 22 or 26 cms. This plant takes some time to begin growth but once started grows well.

Floating plants

These can be used to shade parts of the tank and to provide cover for young fishes, especially those of the top–living livebearers.

Duckweed *(Lemna minor)* is so common that it often finds its way into your aquarium clinging to other plants. It grows fast and will have to be cleared with a net from time to time or it will cover the whole surface like a blanket. The excess, when removed, can be used for feeding to larger fishes, especially large barbs. *Salvinia* is similar to duckweed but has a central stem and the upper surfaces of the leaves bear numerous hairs. Water lettuce *(Pistia stratiotes)* is a much larger plant than both preceding varieties. It has long feathery roots that often reach down to the bottom. It does not seem to do well under artificial light alone. A cover glass is necessary to protect these floating plants from scorching.

Plants of the genus *Ceratopteris* do well under artificial light and may be grown at the surface or anchored in the gravel. Many daughter plants are carried on the leaf edges. These develop and break away as the leaf becomes old and dies.

These are Cryptocoryne *species which do well in the subdued light of an aquarium. Drawings courtesy of Tropica, Denmark.*

Often used as a centre piece are the Amazon sword plants (*Echinodorus*) of which there are both narrow and wide leafed varieties. Both can grow to a height of 45 cm. The leaves are pale green and the young plants are produced on long runners. Amazon swords need bright light to grow well.

Water wisteria (*Synnema triflorum*) is a pale green plant with large leaves that split into fingers very like those of *Ceratopteris*.

Plants of the genus *Bacopa* make a pleasant contrast to those of other varieties. In this group the stem is thick and the leaves small and rounded. They can grow vertically to a height of 30 cm. *Elodea* is really a cold water species but can be used in tropical aquaria. Higher temperatures and strong light do, however, cause it to grow too fast and therefore under these conditions it is necessary to keep cropping it back.

Plants need almost as much care as your fishes, so do not plunge them into cold water as soon as you get them home or allow them to dry out (washing should be done in lukewarm water). Before planting remove dead leaves and any old brown roots and push them into the gravel bed so that the joint between stem and root is level with the surface of the gravel or just above. They may cost slightly more but they will take much more quickly and losses are fewer. Only buy clean, healthy looking plants, not those with many brown leaves or roots. At first your plants will take a little time to start growing because, in a new tank, there will be no sediment in the gravel on which they can feed. This will be rectified soon after the introduction of the fish.

Planting arrangements should be in a horseshoe pattern—rocks to the rear, shorter plants to the front.

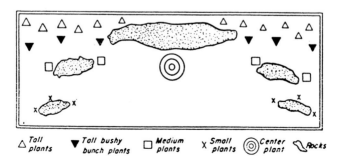

5.
Fishes

All fishes possess fins (some more than others) which enable them to propel themselves in a controlled manner. There are usually seven fins present, four of which are paired. These are the ventral and pectoral fins. The pectorals, which are roughly equivalent to the forelegs of a higher animal, are used for slow movement. They enable the fish to pull itself upward or downward, or, if used sin-

This Geophagus *cichlid is a mouthbrooder. The young go in and out of their parent's mouth until they grow too large to fit!*

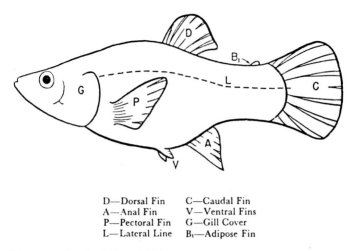

D—Dorsal Fin   C—Caudal Fin
A—Anal Fin   V—Ventral Fins
P—Pectoral Fin   G—Gill Cover
L—Lateral Line   B₁—Adipose Fin

Diagram of typical fins of fishes.

gly, to turn. They are also important braking devices, for slowing down and stopping; a bird uses its wings in the same way.

The pelvic or ventral fins correspond to a higher animal's hind legs and are used as stabilizers to prevent the fish from rolling over. The dorsal fin also performs this function as the fish travels through the water. If two dorsal fins are present, which is sometimes the case, they are known as the anterior and posterior respectively. The dorsal fins are supported by spiny rays in the front whilst those behind are soft and flexible. The anal fin may also have hard and soft rays and is used as a keel when the fish moves forward. The main means of propulsion is the caudal (tail) fin which also acts as a rudder.

Fish may have an external covering of scales, bony plates, or a fine delicate skin, which is always covered by mucus. This layer of mucus not only helps the fish to slide through the water but also protects it from infection, therefore whenever you have to handle fish, make sure you do so with wet hands so as not to damage this delicate membrane.

A fish's eyes are large and positioned so that it can see in all directions. There are no eyelids, so the eyes are always open but protected by tough transparent membranes. Below the eyes are the nostrils which are sensitive over a limited distance; they are also involved with taste. The mouths of fish are adapted to the particular method of feeding. For instance fish that feed on the bottom often have suckers for dealing with algae, while fish fond of feeding at the surface have mouths positioned upward. Food is usually broken up by bony plates in the throat, but some fishes possess sharp teeth.

Behind the gill plates are the delicate gills containing numerous fine blood vessels for the extraction of oxygen from the water. In a few fishes a labyrinth is present behind the mouth which can remove oxygen from air bubbles taken from the surface. In all fishes water is taken in through the mouth and passes over the gills and is then ejected out under the gill plates. Along each side of a fish is a lateral line which consists of modified scales each containing a pore linked to a canal beneath. This system of pores is extremely sensitive and can detect vibrations passing through the water and warn the fish of approaching danger.

Fish possess all the usual internal organs found in other animals but with a very necessary addition—a swim bladder. This is a gas filled organ which functions rather like an air balloon. The amount of gas in the bladder can be regulated to suit the depth at which the fish is swimming. If the bladder is low in gas the fish will sink, if full it will rise. It is rather more complicated than this of course, but basically this is the way in which it works.

A Black Tetra, Gymnocorymbus ternetzi.

Black Ruby Barbs, Puntius nigrofasciatus.

The colour of a fish is dependent on special pigment cells called *chromatophores*. These cells can contract or expand. If a number expand together they produce a coloured spot or stripe. Chromatophores may be present in several different colours so that the fish can present a large range of hues and markings. A fish is able to change its colour to match its surroundings or for courtship or due to fright. Ill health and age also have an effect on colour.

Fish tissues also contain *iridocytes*, formed from waste products, which are highly reflective and give certain parts of the body a many coloured sheen.

When keeping fish it is important to learn their vulnerabilities so as to avoid being unintentionally cruel.

All fish are very receptive to vibrations, so it is important to move carefully around the tank when doing odd jobs. Be careful not to knock the glass; certainly do not tap it to attract the attention of the fish; all this will succeed in doing is to frighten them into diving for cover. Fishes subjected to this kind of treatment will become very nervous, go off their food and hide for most of the time. Another cause of nervousness is brought on by the sudden change from dark to light when the lights are switched on in the morning. As fish have no eyelids they must have time to adjust their eyes to light gradually. Therefore, if the room is in darkness, switch on the room light first, a little while before the tank lights. Tropical fishes can adapt themselves to quite a wide range of temperatures, but they cannot endure sudden changes in temperature, so be careful when moving fishes from one tank to another. Be careful also when catching fishes; use patience and do not chase the fish all round the tank until it becomes exhausted. Use two nets, one in conjunction with the other and you will find the job relatively easy. Top-living fishes can be caught by gently bringing the net up from beneath them.

Bullying is a common problem, so always watch out for this. If you see it occurring remove the culprit immediately. Do not overcrowd your tank as this causes a lack of oxygen and a great excess of sediment which in turn can can cause sicknesses such as tuberculosis.

At some time it may be necessary to kill a fish. The simplest and most humane way to do this is to throw it hard onto the ground, which usually kills it instantly.

This bully is the African cichlid Tropheus moorii.

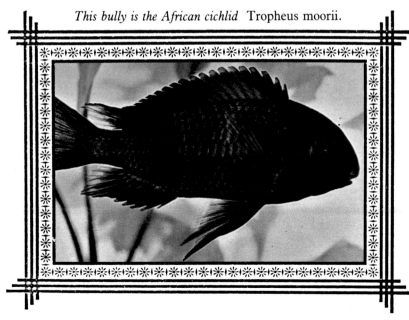

A lovely pair of longfinned Black Swordtails, Xiphophorus helleri. *They are livebearers.*

6.
Livebearing Fishes

Livebearing toothcarp, collectively known as "livebearers", are often the beginner's first choice when considering a community tank. Many features contribute to their suitability. For one thing they are good community fish and will take almost any type of food. Their relatively small size makes it possible to keep several specimens together in a fairly small tank, and they can be obtained in a scintil-

This female Guppy has just delivered the youngster which she is about to eat!

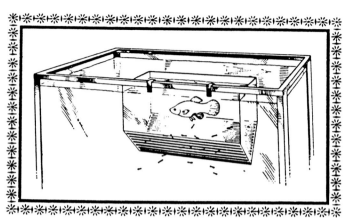

A livebearer in a breeding trap which allows the young to fall through the slotted bottom, out of the cannibalistic reaches of their mother!!

lating variety of colours. Lastly they are hardy and even breed fairly readily in a community aquarium.

Livebearers are found all over the New World in widely differing environments—from stagnant freshwater ponds choked with weeds to the brackish water of river mouths. In the aquarium they prove extremely adaptable and special conditions are unnecessary.

The main distinguishing feature of the livebearer is the gonopodium which is a special development of the anal fin in the male fish. When the fish is about half grown this fin develops into a grooved, rodlike organ used by the male to implant the sperm into the female. Unlike the egglayers, the eggs of livebearers develop inside the female and the young are born alive and well formed. This special anal fin of the male therefore makes sexing of livebearers a simple matter. This organ, which is normally pointed backwards, can be twisted sideways and forward to enter the female's vent.

When several livebearers of the same species are kept together the males will soon begin to display to the females, and it is then that they show themselves off to their best. If observed closely the male will be seen to dart up behind the female where mating will take place. After fertilisation the lower part of the female's body gradually becomes enlarged and a dark patch will appear at the base of the tail. This is called the gravid spot and is, of course, caused by the developing fishes. The young are born thirty to forty days after mating. Although only up to 1.3 cm in length the baby livebearer is longer than its egglaying counterpart. It immediately swims off in search of cover among the plants or hides amongst the gravel on the bottom of the tank. The fry can easily be fed on powdered dry foods etc.

Because the females are able to store the male sperm inside them it is possible for them to produce up to six broods from one mating, and also to have in one brood young from different male parents. The size of the brood will vary from species to species, in relation to the size of the parents and the conditions in which it lives. The latter also affects the gestation period. It should be remembered when breeding livebearers that any fish in the same tank with a mouth large enough will not hesitate to devour the newly born young, and this even goes for fish of the same species since all live-bearers are unpleasantly cannibalistic. Neither are the parents averse to a tasty morsel of their own brood. It is best therefore to place the gravid female in a breeding trap, usually constructed of fine mesh stretched over a light square frame. It is best to put both trap and female in a separate tank with the trap suspended from the back or sides of the aquarium. The mesh should be large enough to allow the fry to escape into the main tank and out of reach of mother's jaws. A few fronds of *Cabomba* or some similar feathery plant will make the growing fish feel more secure.

A beautiful male Guppy.

Guppy
Poecilia reticulata 3.2 cm - 4.4 cm
Trinidad

The guppy is probably the best known of all beginner's fish. It is active and exceptionally hardy. In fact, though often used as an aquatic guinea pig, these little fish remain completely oblivious to rough handling and even have the audacity to breed under the most trying conditions. Sexual dimorphism in the guppy is developed to a high degree and therefore one might be forgiven for thinking that the male and female belong to different species. The adult female, for one thing, is larger than the male by a good half inch and is a rather nondescript grey or dull gold. (The female in the so-called golden strain may bear some tail colour.) In contrast the wild male bears a profusion of patches and spots of almost every colour, and it is interesting to note that no two males are identical.

As a community fish the guppy is hard to beat. It is placid, though not timid and it is always on the move and continually displaying to the females. Although this species originates in Trinidad, its range has been artificially extended to exploit its potential as a larvicidal fish (to eat mosquito larvae). Its usefulness is due greatly to its breeding potential. It is not unusual for a large female to pro-

A female Guppy in the actual act of having a baby!

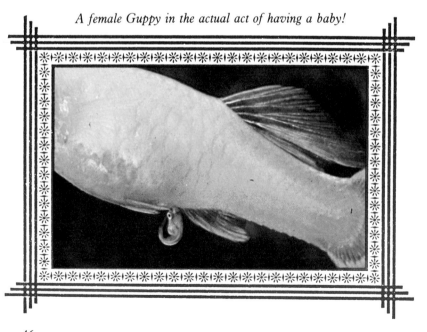

46

A Hi-fin Variegated Swordtail.

duce fifty babies, and the young grow rapidly, as many as four broods being raised in one year. No special conditions are necessary to breed guppies. As long as the pH is about average guppies will breed freely. Ideally water temperature should be around 25°C. If a higher temperature is provided this will induce faster breeding.

Swordtail
Xiphophorus helleri 10.2 cm Mexico

Due to its prolific nature the swordtail is a popular and inexpensive fish. Its common name derives from the sword-like extension of the lower tail fin in the male fish. Apart from this the sexes are alike and both grow to about four inches in length, excluding sword.

Like the guppy its mouth is directed upward for surface feeding. Dried foods are eagerly taken, though it is not averse to scavenging and likes a little algae which it pecks from the aquarium walls and plant leaves. Large males are inclined to bully and so the swordtail is best kept with other robust species. The original colour of this fish in the wild is green with a rusty zig-zagging line along the side of the body. However, nowadays the red variety, being the most popular, is more often seen. A vast number of colour varieties are now available, including the tuxedo swordtail in which the whole lower half of the body is black.

The males are ardent courtiers often darting backwards six or more inches to impress the females. Fertility is high, a brood often containing up to two hundred and fifty babies. The young are about 0.6 cm when born and are easy to rear to full size if given plenty of food and, more important, space to grow. Breeding swordtails prefer a water at neutral pH or just slightly alkaline. Temperature should be about 25°C.

A pair of Red Platies, X. maculatus.

Platy
Xiphophorus maculatus 5.1 cm - 6.3 cm Mexico

Here we have another Mexican fish, well known as the platy and of great similarity to the swordtail. The body is just a little shorter and deeper and the male possesses no sword. It is a placid fish and always displays itself well in any open portion of the tank. Colour varieties are even more numerous than in the swordtail and many of these follow the same lines. All are obtained by selective breeding and hybridization from the original strain which was known as the "moonfish" because of a dark moon-shaped mark at the base of the tail. Due to selective breeding, however, few of them nowadays have this mark so pronounced.

They are prolific but breed less rapidly than the swordtail and are less hardy. The young develop their colour gradually, being green to brown at birth, and take up to a year to achieve full colour.

Platies prefer slightly alkaline water for breeding and a temperature of 25°C.

Molly
Poecilia sphenops 7.5 cm - 10.25 cm
North and Central South America

The hardiest of the mollies is the short-finned species, of which there are numerous varieties. It is not the easiest of livebearers to keep, since in the wild it lives in brackish water. The addition of salt (one teaspoon to the litre) in the aquarium does much to improve their general health whilst a certain amount of algae on which to feed is to be recommended.

Mollies breed best in a well planted tank. They are less inclined to cannibalism than most fish and therefore the plants should supply the fry with adequate cover in which to hide. Breeding mollies prefer a high temperature of about 26°C and the water should be slightly alkaline.

A Sailfin Black Molly, Poecilia sphenops.

A pair of Dwarf Gouramis in a spawning embrace. The eggs will float up into the nest of floating aquatic plants.

7.
Egglaying Fishes

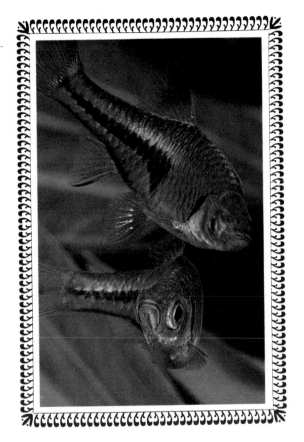

The egglayers comprise a large group which vary enormously in shape and habit. There are also great differences in the way they breed and the care they take of their young. Some, such as barbs scatter their eggs and their parental responsibility stops. Others drop slightly adhesive eggs, while others, the gouramis for instance, build bubble nests and protect them from intruders. Cichlids also

The very colorful Rasbora hengeli.

protect their eggs which are frequently laid on the walls or roof of a cave. The parents often fan the eggs to keep the water around them fresh.

Egglaying fish are more difficult to breed than livebearers, usually needing a separate tank and carefully controlled conditions, but it should not be thought that this is beyond the scope of the beginner. All that is needed is a little knowledge and, more important, care and patience. Unfortunately the scope of this book is too limited to go very deeply into breeding egglayers, so only a general guide will be given for each group.

Cyprinidae

This family of fishes is one of the largest in the world, containing over 1,500 species. Members of this group are found in many parts of the world, including Europe, Asia, Africa and North America. The size range within the family is considerable, our little aquarium fishes having cousins which are measured in feet. Many of these fishes have whisker-like appendages around the mouth to aid in the search for food. These "barbels" are sensitive organs of taste and touch. The mouth does not bear teeth and the food is ground by a plate of bone situated in the throat. The body itself bears large scales and is usually of a conventional fish shape. A distinguishing

Botia striata. *Photo by Hansen.*

Rasbora heteromorpha *spawning by laying their eggs underneath a* Cryptocoryne *leaf.*

feature of this group is the lack of an adipose fin. The Cyprinidae are also particularly fast moving fish. The main group within this family is represented by the genera *Capoeta, Puntius* and *Barbodes* (barbs), *Labeo* (sharks) and the subfamily *Rasborinae.*

Barbs

Barbs have always been popular community fish. There are many species which only grow to about 5 cm and as many again which reach 7.6 cm or more; the latter of course need large tanks if they are to thrive. The following pages include in the main the smaller barbs as these fish are particularly suitable for a community tank. These fish are generally peaceful though they are not shy and tend to display themselves well at the front of the tank with fins well spread. Although they prefer slightly acid water and temperatures of around 25°C they are very adaptable and most tank setups will be satisfactory. They do, however, need plenty of space and prefer a well aerated tank. When transporting barbs do not crowd them otherwise the resultant lack of oxygen will quickly cause their deaths. Barbs are fish of the Old World where they are widespread, living in shoals in rivers and lakes. In the wild they eat a lot of plant material and in the aquarium are apt to nibble the softer plants. The growth of a certain amount of duckweed on the water surface is beneficial, especially for the larger varieties.

The Red-tailed Black Shark, Labeo bicolor.

Labeos

Labeos are usually known as sharks, but this is due entirely to their appearance; they are in no way related to their fearsome marine namesakes. They are found in Africa and from India through Burma and Thailand to Indonesia. Labeos prefer slightly alkaline water and will eat most foods. The mouth is specialised for scavenging and for scooping algae off the rocks.

Rasborinae (subfamily)

The fish contained in this subfamily vary greatly in size and appearance. The smaller ones are highly coloured and peaceful, making them suitable companions for other small community fish such as tetras. They have a wide natural range which stretches through S.E. Asia to China, the East Indies and the Philippines. Most of those imported come from around the Malay Peninsula.

Rasbora do best in slightly acid water (a pH of 6.5 is ideal) if they are to breed. In a breeding tank the depth of the water should be about 15 cm and the temperature 24°C-26°C. Clumps of peat fibre should be placed in the water and in these the semi-adhesive eggs will be laid. A breeding trap is not recommended for these fish. The eggs hatch in about three days and the fry need egg yolk emulsion followed later by brine shrimp.

Characidae

Most of the fishes in this family come from tropical Africa and Central and South America. The most popular aquarium species originate in the lakes and rivers of the Amazon Basin. Heavy rainfall in these areas washes minerals out of the soil leaving water which is very much like distilled water. In the wild these fish are found in large shoals in waters which maintain warm temperatures. It is clear, therefore, that in the aquarium they do best if kept together in numbers. Most characins possess teeth and an adipose fin. All of them have at least one of these features. There are extremely wide variations in size, shape and habit within the family. They range from the large and devious piranha to the smaller tetras which are peaceful, fragile little fish. The smaller fish can be mixed with any fish of similar size.

To breed characins one needs a soft water aquarium with a bottom layer entirely of peat. The water temperature should be approximately 28°C. The sexes should be kept separate until well fed and then placed in a darkened tank. When they have spawned the parents should be removed but the tank kept in darkness. The fry, which take a day to hatch, hang vertically at the surface. After a few days they start to swim in a horizontal position and can now be fed. A good commercial food is suitable.

The Cardinal Tetra, Paracheirodon axelrodi.

Aplocheilus lineatus.

Cyprinodontidae (Killifishes)

The killifishes are a large family of egglayers closely related to the livebearing toothcarps. They possess teeth and are often called egglaying toothcarps.

Included in this family is a group called panchax, many of which are particularly colourful. They are rather tubular in shape and have large jaws. Larger ones can easily swallow fishes the size of male guppies and therefore should only be kept with fishes their own size. Almost all species swim just below the surface of the water and can detect anything passing above them with a "third eye" and dive to safety. This "eye" represented by a light coloured area and most pronounced in *A. lineatus*, is in fact only rudimentary and through it the fish has no real sight, but it can detect light and shade. When catching these fish it is therefore best to bring the net slowly up from below, trapping the fish at the surface before the net is detected. As the panchax are good jumpers a well fitted cover glass is essential. In the aquarium they will take dried foods although they appreciate the occasional live tid-bit. The panchax come from Africa, India, Indonesia and Ceylon.

56

Cichlidae (Cichlids)

These fishes are found in lakes and other sluggish waters in many parts of the world. Although they tend to be rather aggressive they are quite easy to breed and take good care of their young. A general method of breeding is to place the pair in a large tank supplied with deep sand and some smooth rocks—a half flower pot will supply a good cover, which some cichlids prefer. Plants need not be provided as these will only be uprooted when the parents dig their holes in which to keep the young. The eggs are laid around a stone which has been previously cleaned by the parents. Both parents now fan the eggs in turn until they hatch. The newly hatched fry are kept in a depression made in the sand where they are protected for the first few days of life. When they are about half an inch long it is best to remove the parents as a few of the fry may get eaten. They should be fed on brine shrimp for the first week and later on mealworms and fine dried food. Adult cichlids of the larger species are often predacious on other fishes.

Cichlids like to choose their own mates and so if you wish to breed them it is best to buy several half grown specimens and keep them until a couple pair up and mature. Males can be identified by the long points to the fins and brighter colours.

Microgeophagus ramirezi *laying eggs on a flat stone.*

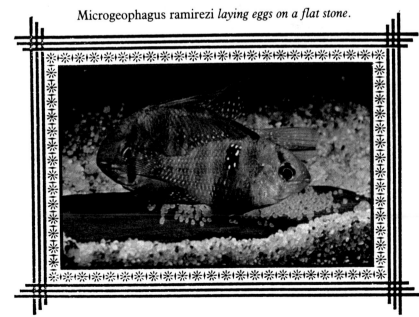

Anabantidae

This family includes the gouramis and bettas. They all possess an ancillary breathing organ called the labyrinth and are often referred to as labyrinth fishes. This organ is contained in a sack at the back of the gill chamber and has well supplied blood vessels on its surface. Air gulped in through the mouth is passed into the labyrinth where the oxygen is in turn passed into the blood. Used air is pushed out under the gill plates by the next gulp of air. The advantage of this organ is that the Anabantidae can live in water containing less oxygen than other groups of fishes, i.e. stagnant water. If you observe a labyrinth fish you will see it rise for air at intervals. These intervals are, of course, shorter when the fish is active than when it is resting.

Most of the labyrinth fishes are bubble-nest builders. The nest is formed from bubbles of air which the male coats with saliva and places at the surface. He then proceeds to attract the female beneath the nest whilst driving all other fish away. In this position the male embraces the female and squeezes her body. This action of squeezing releases a few eggs. As they fall both fish collect them in their mouths one by one. They are then coated with saliva, encased in a bubble of air and placed in the nest. This process is repeated until all the eggs are laid.

The Pearl Gourami, one of the most popular anabantoids.

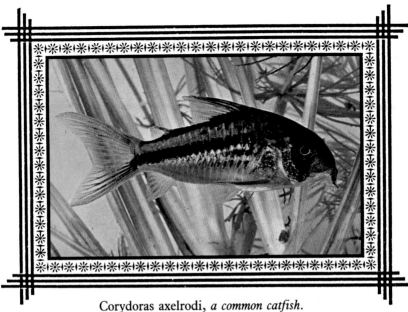

Corydoras axelrodi, *a common catfish.*

Callichthyidae

The fishes in this family are catfish with long plates on the flanks. By far the most popular catfish are those in the genus *Corydoras*. Most catfish are great scavengers and do a tremendous amount to keep the tank clean.

Mochokidae

This is an interesting family of upside down catfish containing several species.

Cobitidae (Loaches and Botias)

The fishes in this family are found in much of Asia and Europe, with a few in Africa. They are rather elongated in shape and live on or beneath the mud of pools. Mainly they are scavengers and can be very useful in the aquarium, seeking out scraps of food with the aid of their barbels. They have no teeth but some species do possess sharp spines just below the eyes. These spines are for protection and normally lie flat, but care should be taken when catching them as the spines tend to get caught up in nets. It is bet to use a plain material net rather than the normal mesh net.

8.
Diseases

Prevention is better than cure and therefore the best way to combat disease is to stop it before it gets into the tank. This means quarantine just before they are introduced to the main aquarium. For this, of course, you will need a spare tank in which all newly purchased fish are kept for at least two weeks. This should allow plenty of time for infectious diseases to manifest themselves.

White Spot (*Ichthyophthirius*)

This is by far the most common disease of aquarium fish and is often met with in newly imported specimens; it is highly infectious and will soon contaminate every fish in the tank. An infected fish will be seen to rub itself against rocks and the gravel bed of the tank to remove irritation. When examined the fish will be seen to bear tiny white spots. These usually occur first on the fins but soon spread to the body and even into the gills. The spots are caused by a minute parasite which burrows into the skin forming small white cysts. Unless quickly treated the fish will become covered with these spots and die. Luckily many good cures are available. Those containing malachite green are perhaps the most effective. The

This fish is infected with White Spot (Ich).

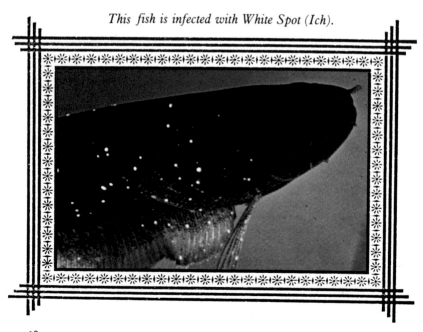

This Hemigrammus *has fungus growing on its head.*

temperature of the tank may be raised to 28°C to speed up the process. It is usually best to treat the whole tank rather than take the infected fish out because if one fish is infected others will be also, even if this is not immediately apparent.

Velvet Disease (*Oodinium*)

This disease manifests itself as yellow pin point spots which give the effect of a covering of yellow velvet. It occurs much less frequently than white spot and good cures are available.

Fungus

Most fungal infections can be treated with sea salt. This may be added to the water at a rate of one teaspoon of salt per gallon of water and increased to two spoonfuls after two days. A fresh solution should be used every day until the cure is complete. If the fungus is heavy and localised as in the case of mouth fungus, the fish can be treated individually. The lips of the fish should be swabbed gently with a fine cloth soaked in strong salt solution, and the fish quickly returned to the tank. Many good antifungal drugs are available at petshops.

1. *Siamese Fighting fish*, **Betta splendens**; 2. **Rasbora heteromorpha**; 3. *Pearl Danio*, **Brachydanio albolineatus**. *Photo by Burkhard Kahl.*

PHOTOGRAPHY
Dr.Herbert R.Axelrod: 27,41,55,59; Frickhinger:60;
H.Hansen:56; Burkhard Kahl: 2-3,62-63; Dr.Karl Knaack:39;
Kurt Quitschau:47; Hans Joachim Richter: 5,7,19,24,37,43,
46,50,51,53,57,58; Andre Roth: 25,42; G.J.M.Timmerman:40;
Gene Wolfsheimer: 48; Ruda Zukal: 31,61.